Fractions of a Poet!c Soul

Copyright © 2025 by Ranjit Roi
All Rights Reserved

mattabesset@gmail.com

Cover Illustration by Aubren

ISBN: 978-1-7367772-9-9

Fractions of a Poet!c Soul

by

Ranjit Roi

≈ Mattabesset ≈

*To my dad, who planted
a seed of a dreamer ins!de me
and nurtured it.*

*To a pa!nter who pa!nted
the fract!ons of the dream;
To an author who pr!nted
them into pages.*

*F!ona Beltran Wh!ting
Mark Van Horne*

*And to the readers who breathe
Life into these pages,
Thank you.*

*It is true, dreams
come true. Hence proved.*

Contents

Preface...*ix*
Fractions of a Poet!c Soul............................*xi*

Fractions of Love

Fades Away... 3
Maybe 5
Barefoot 7
L!ke 9
Sonnet I... 11
So Many But One 13
Half of the T!me 15
You're An Art....................................... 17
I Mean Love 19
Love Undy!ng 21
Ode to Beauty 23
Respect and Then Love............................. 25
At F!rst S!ght 27
Forget Me Not, Please.............................. 29
F!nal Date... 31
A Fallen Leaf 33
Let Me Hold Your Hand 35
A Car!ng One....................................... 37
She is a Beauty 39
Merma!dika 41
A Bl!nd Boy's Dream............................... 43
A Girl in P!nk and Blue 45
You Came to Me 47
The Art of Moonl!ght 49

Eclipse

For They Forgot	53
Stage	55
Be!ng Real	57
Purpose of Poets	59
A Typewr!ter	61
The World of Humans	63
A Person	65
Poet's Shoes	67
Colorbl!nd	69

Fractions of Life

Fa!led in a Way	73
L!bra	75
Feel	77
Pa!nting the Bubbles	79
Anonymous	81
Ode to the Ra!n	83
If I Were an Alphabet	85
Time Travel with Art	87
Not a Poet	89
Apology to Beauty	91
Mag!c	93
A Man's Fa!th	95
Why So Ser!ous	97
Unseen V!sions	99
The G!ft of Autumn	101
Ink Speaks to Me	103
Noth!ng 'More or Less'	105
Anonymous II	107
Ode to October	109

Preface

I love nature, art, and life. I convey my words to paint pictures of how I feel and how nature itself makes me feel. Mostly, how I see the world. I share my emotions with you through my poems, hoping for my readers to find this book a balm for the soul.

I am pleased to share my poems to ignite your inner romantic and artist with a little glint of humor; a gentle reminder that each of us is unique and creative.

Ranjit Roi

Fractions of a Poet!c Soul

A walk!ng m!racle w!th pen and paper
Mag!cal error in grammar and l!terature
The little 'i' of surpr!se
Someth!ng for all the poets
To laugh and sm!le about
No doubt, he's fool like a w!se
And w!se l!ke a fool
One m!nute star!ng at the clouds
Next m!nute float!ng w!th them
Measur!ng the length and breath and
Alt!tude of sol!tude
Letters, words and patterns
Calculat!on of compass!onated
compass!on, the fine line between
Time and imag!nation
Fract!ons of the soul
From the very bottom
Sprouting l!ke the petals
Of cherry blossom.

Fractions of Love

Fades Away

We seemed so far
But far too close
For the roses of our love
Will always be in blossom
Whether it is spr!ng w!nter or autumn

Time w!ll pass and seasons change
Memor!es fade away
Feel!ng w!ll change too
People w!ll leave
But, the heart never forgets

L!ke once you were a sm!le on my face
Now, you are in the tears of my eyes.
I'm sorry it's not easy to forget
And I can't g!ve away
At least, not in th!s l!fe.

Maybe

Love, maybe a dream
In which !'m fallen in
Sw!ft and slow float!ng
L!ke a paper boat
Wh!spering secret thoughts
Try!ng to put them in words
You and me, maybe
Fract!ons of the same verse
And rest I just trust the un!verse

Love, maybe a delus!on
Tangled between real!ty and imag!nation
Into an ocean of emot!ons
This soul can hope and m!nd can h!de
But the eyes... eyes could never l!e
And every t!me I see you sm!le it feels l!ke
!'m liv!ng a dream I was dream!ng
Someday, maybe I w!ll introduce you
To the world as my bride

Love, maybe it's all in my head
Every word you sa!d, every moment
We shared is l!ke a tattoo in my bra!n
Some are meant to fall in love
With each other but not meant
To be together...
Maybe you're a feel!ng I feel forever
Maybe !'m always a f!ne dreamer
And a fool lover!

Barefoot

Barefoot on tip of her toes
She stands tall
Fingers laced up
And fists aga!nst the wall

Eyes f!lled with wonder lust
Try!ng to h!de her sensual love
But, with every breath
She is los!ng herself
More than enough

Everyth!ng seems to stop for a wh!le
When her l!ps melt w!th m!ne
The moment of pure bl!ss
And the beauty of our first k!ss.

L!ke

L!ke I l!ke the way you l!ke me
And I l!ke the way I l!ke you
I l!ke, you are l!ke that
And I l!ke, I am l!ke this
Maybe in your dreams
You w!shed about me
And in my dreams
I w!shed about you
And it came true…
I am more l!ke you
And less l!ke me
And you are more l!ke me
And less l!ke you
Maybe that's what happens
When someone l!ke you… l!ke you
And we both knew…
You are another version of me
And I am another version of you…

Sonnet I

A dreamer, maybe a fool
Who doesn't know to pretend but
Clouds and the w!nds, stars and the moon
Pen and paper always been his fr!end
Never did he indulge in procrastinat!on
The joy of think!ng has no end
A combinat!on of vis!on and imaginat!on
These thoughts, the verse, and the rhymes
Keep flow!ng l!ke snow is snow!ng
W!nd is blow!ng, leaves are danc!ng
B!rds sing!ng and I'm writ!ng
An ode to the pa!nting
While Mona L!sa is star!ng and smil!ng
L!ke an empress, a poetess, my M!stress.

So Many But One

Some have the prett!est sm!le
Some just whisper ins!de bra!n
And talk with s!gns
Some have fabulous ha!rstyle
Some have snow wh!te sk!n
Some have great sense of dress!ng
Some very shy and melt l!ke candle
Some are very innocent and sensit!ve
And among all I saw you
Shy eyes and a s!mple sm!le
Noth!ng spec!al like others
Noth!ng to compare but st!ll
Pure, vibrant and rare
And my heart chooses you
And it w!ll keep choos!ng you
Every today every tomorrow
Till the end of t!me.

Half of the T!me

Half of the t!me I lie saying !'m fine
Half of the t!me !'m a lost soul
And th!nk if I could rewr!te the stars
Rearrange the l!nes in palm of the hand
Surgery the heart and the m!nd
So, I could forget all these scars

Half of the t!me !'m frag!le like a snow flake
Half of the t!me !'m s!lent sad l!ke a lake
And th!nk if I could rew!nd t!me
Undo the th!ngs I've done
Shouldn't have sm!led back to the sm!le
Shouldn't have poured my heart
Shouldn't have bel!eved the wh!te lies
But, st!ll I can't deny I'll never forget you
At least not in th!s l!fe

Half of the t!me tears roll down my face
Half of the t!me I pray for your happ!ness
For memor!es know no boundar!es
Even when !'m los!ng, !'m winn!ng
And I'll never give up
Because if I do it is not love
!'m stardust and I know it's hard
To find a lover
When you're a poet!c dreamer.

You're An Art

For you're an art, versat!le and infin!te
The best of the beauteous k!nd
Insight of an ethereal m!nd, O

You're the most beaut!ful color
That the pa!nt brush has ever touched
And the only pa!nting without any flaws

You're the most beaut!ful thought
That has found the word
And the only mean!ngful poetry I've got

You're the most beaut!ful song
That my m!nd keeps play!ng on and on
And the only th!ng that stays
when everyth!ng is gone

You're the most beaut!ful flower
That blooms w!th every season
And the only reason for butterflies
and bees creat!on

You're everywhere l!ke the clouds
You're everywhere l!ke the wind
You're everywhere l!ke the sky

And among all the stars
You're the only one that's worth
L!ke the moon to earth.

I Mean Love

Between the depths of the sea
And the h!ghness of the sky
I wander with the clouds
I love w!sdom and compass!on
wise soul and genuine kindness
nature and its beauty
pass!on of poetry
love at f!rst s!ght
soul connect!on
deep conversat!on
be!ng in love
be!ng not so cool
be!ng a poet!c fool.

Love Undy!ng

Down on my knees
Truly a fool talk!ng to the moon
W!shing if there could be
A handsome, smart and cool
Guy ins!de me, but I lack all three
Forg!ve me God please
Be!ng d!rt, ! feel in love w!th an angel
Days past and n!ghts lost
Every s!ngle moment I th!nk about her
All I see is butterfl!es and firefl!es
Though I'm so alone, it's my fault
I never knew she's a deja vu
Her voice st!ll echo!ng inside my head
Like the most beaut!ful symphony
I had ever heard ... but now she's gone
To be loved by her is l!ke a day dream!ng
Left me with a bless!ng
Griev!ng and trouble with breath!ng
Suffer!ng when I'm sleep!ng
And miss!ng when we were talk!ng and
Cuddl!ng and kiss!ng and hugg!ng
We were inseparable at one t!me and
My love for you is undy!ng
But, now love showed me it's true mean!ng
Every love story has adorable beginn!ng
And not all have happy end!ng.

Ode to Beauty

The summer as the sun sh!nes
On the waterfall, noth!ng old, noth!ng new,
    everyth!ng p!cturesque
The spr!ng as the fragrance
Of daisies and b!rd's song
M!ngled in the air
The autumn as a walk
On the carpet of leaves to the
Orchards filled with v!nes
The w!nter as warm f!re
And ra!nbow fall!ng w!th the snow
Beneath a Chr!stmas tree
Just you and me
Each t!ck of the clock
Each day of the year
! fell for you
L!ke !'m breath!ng you
Never was ! so al!ve
Unt!l you walked into my l!fe
L!ke a blend of nature and beauty
W!th heart and soul
! pray may be one day
You be parallel on the other s!de
With a sm!le and ! could
Hold your hand and say…
You're the ode to beauty
Living ins!de me.

Respect and Then Love

A guy who flirts with you every t!me
Always th!nking to steal your virg!nity
Is good for you,
But, a guy who always care about you
Treat you l!ke an angel
Is a fool to you.

A guy who is already in relationsh!p
Talks too much fake th!ngs
And you w!ll feel he is perfect
But, a guy who is l!ttle shy
Talks less just because
He respects you
Is a dumb to you.

A good guy rema!ned s!ngle
Just because he is 30% shy
20% he is scared of los!ng you
And 50% he respects all girls
For everyone comes from girls
Who we call mother...
Respect for carry!ng and protect!ng
And love for bringing into
This beautiful world.

At F!rst S!ght

I cannot tell you
How I feel
When I saw you
At f!rst s!ght
If Angels are real
You must be the one
A beauty w!th an en!gmatic sm!le
S!lent l!ps and talk!ng eyes
To you I lost everyth!ng I have
Within me I cannot f!nd myself
Every moment I see you
I feel l!ke I'm blessed
It's not just a co!ncidence or fate
But a part of Cup!d's consp!racy I guess.

Forget Me Not, Please

! always thought, you're ins!de me and
Understand me l!ke no one ever does
! always thought you're ma sky
You're ma stars and ma full moon.
! always thought you're the mag!c
In ma sk!n, bones, and soul
! always thought to bought you
Flowers, honey, and cards and
Make you feel what ! feel for you.
! always thought to get lost w!th you
!nto the world of daisies, dandelions,
Butterfl!es, b!rds, and lakes.
! always thought to make you sm!le
With letters, postcards, and envelopes
Full of symphon!es and poetries.
! always thought to walk w!th you
M!les and m!les until our legs hurt and
we s!t lean!ng on each other's shoulder
! always thought to sleep on your lap
Feeling your waterfall l!ke hair fall!ng
On ma face flawlessly and getting drowned in
    your ocean eyes.
! always thought, you'll forget me not
But, you d!d, plant!ng seeds of sorrow inside
    me...
Now, !'m lost in deep sea
Can't sw!m, can't fly
'Cause you ripped off ma fins and ma w!ngs
And st!ll you're too bl!nd to see
You mean a world to me!

F!nal Date

F!nally I made a f!nal date
To go on a date w!th my date
It's not by m!stake we met
Maybe it was already dec!ded by fate
I th!nk and she th!nks she knows me
But I've got so much to show her yet
Let's not break the connect!on we make
I may be a fool but not fake
W!th you I can create a whole new world
And unfurl the flags of love, peace, and compass!on
Hold my hand and walk w!th me
To a place where the sky and the sea meet
Underneath the magical moon
Let me look at you and keep look!ng
At you unt!l the new day begins
And I know it's the season of spr!ng
The blue sky with cotton candy l!ke clouds
The color of the flowers
The song of the b!rds
And buzz!ng of the bees
And for the rest of l!fe
You and I are butterfly
And every day is cherry blossom.

A Fallen Leaf

A fallen leaf
A soul's broken strings
Feelings and words with wings
Like a discarded greeting card
That has never been adored
Spring has come and gone
With no sign of return
Autumn has arrived making me feel
More and more less alive
The happiness and grief of
A fallen leaf — bruised and broken
Ocean of love left unspoken
Once we sang together with the birds
Once we danced together with the breeze
Once we cuddled together and counted stars
Once we spread the fragrance of love together
I wish I could make it better
With you I want a life a bit little longer
Not ready for this metamorphosis
Happiness turning into emptiness
And how fool of me 'cause I never knew
Love has a darkside too
Like the moon.

Let Me Hold Your Hand

Let me hold your hand
Let me touch your soul
Let me be your s!ght
For th!s moment
Have fa!th in me
I will never let you down
Walk w!th my steps ton!ght
Because ton!ght is the n!ght
The moon is so rare, beaut!ful and br!ght
But not more than
The one by my s!de.

A Car!ng One

The words pour
Rhythm of the heart str!ngs
After be!ng touched by a soul
Like it never happened before.

A soul s!mple car!ng and shy
Left her vo!ce echo!ng ins!de my head
And her face keeps com!ng
Every t!me I close my eyes.

She knows better
I only pretend to be a fr!end
But, too bl!nd to see
She means the world to me.

She is a Beauty

Shall I call those eyes
The m!rror of the blue sky
Shall I lose my all
To that mesmer!zing sm!le
Shall I rejo!ce myself
Every t!me I hear her vo!ce
Shall I hold her hands
That color the snowflakes.

Shall I walk by her side
For she is always
Pure, v!brant and new
Shall I put my hands on her hands
And l!sten to her deep self
Shall I be the shoulder to lean on
When she is m!les away from home
Shall I g!ve her what my father
Gave to a woman
Who I call my mother
Respect, trust, and never-end!ng love.

But, no matter how much I praise
It is never enough
For I was darkness and ra!n
She came l!ke sunsh!ne
And created ra!nbows in my l!fe.

Merma!dika

O, dear sky h!gh
Do not just stare at me
You have so many attendants
Send one of thee and tell her
How much I m!ss her.

O, dear m!ghty moon
Do not just stand at that he!ght
Come closer for a wh!le
And blow a l!ttle more l!ght
So I can see her mesmer!zing sm!le
By your s!de.

O, dear w!nter w!nds
Do not be so cold-hearted
I know she's cold and alone
Go and blow a l!ttle slow
And g!ve her the warmness of my soul.

O, dear Merma!dika
We seemed so far
But, we are far too close
For the roses of our love
Will always be in blossom
Whether it is spr!ng w!nter or autumn.

A Bl!nd Boy's Dream

My mistress who I know
Only by her name
And the sweet vo!ce
That talks innocent words
Reminds me of fa!ry angels.

Though I never met her
Nor d!d I touch her soft hands
But still I can feel
The fragrance of her sk!n
And hear the sound of her laugh.

It was the cold month of December
With orch!ds in my hand
And shyness in my eyes
I saw her with red and black dress
And a simple sm!le on her face
Makes me so h!gh
I st!ll remember.

I do want to go further
And take her to my favor!te place
Where p!ne trees, chirp!ng b!rds
And chilling w!nds accompany us
But, I hes!tate, so do my emot!ons
'Cause I never want to let her go
And what she th!nks
I did not know.

A Girl in P!nk and Blue

The moment I saw you
I thought of all the beaut!ful songs
But none can match your beauty
I'm confused and mesmer!zed
At the same t!me
Are you an art of imag!nation?
Or God's most beaut!ful creat!on?

You're such a beauty
Even mermaids are very much jealous
You're so natural l!ke the lotus
Has given you her pur!ty
You're so prec!ous l!ke
Dew drops on rose petals.

Everyt!me I see you
You're br!ght v!brant and new
A perfect angel in p!nk and blue
But, I'm sorry
I cannot find any words
So true that can descr!be
The hands that have created you.

You Came to Me

You came to me
L!ke the g!ft of Chr!stmas
L!ke the one I always w!shed for
Pure, s!mple and lov!ng
From deep w!thin
Scatter!ng the l!ght
That's br!ghtening my m!nd
And enl!ghtening my soul
L!ke it never happened before
W!th your sm!le I sh!ne
For you are truly one of a k!nd.

The Art of Moonl!ght

I l!ve I love I d!e
I w!sh I could express or describe
Half of the time of my life
I think about you and me and us
And our poetic universe
I wish I could have known
You're a dream I cannot afford
I wish I could reverse the time
With a verse and make you feel
The feeling we felt
On the day we first met
Falling for you was not a mistake
I may be a fool but not fake
You're an art of which
I'm a faded part now
But somehow I'm happy
The way you happened in my life
L!ke the moonl!ght
You brightened my mind
Enlightened my soul
And ingrained in my blood and bones
Not all can feel, not all can see
A l!ving poetry ins!de me.

Eclipse

For They Forgot

Dreaming, thinking and inking
Inking, thinking and dreaming
Till the Heart's beating
Lungs breathing and eyes blinking
This soul is a poetry
This body is a painting
The world around has cut off my wings
And dragged me down into the dirt
But they forgot
For the sky I'm bird
For the water I'm flood
For the the sand I'm cactus
For the mud I'm lotus
And for the paper I'm ink filled with blood.

Stage

Since I'm in a posit!on
For I th!nk I'm here w!th a reason
New a!r, new water and new season

I tr!ed and I'm try!ng
To blend in w!th the
Th!ngs around me
That it's total hypocrisy
That I can clearly see

I used to be a free b!rd
I wandered with the clouds
I used to walk but my m!nd fl!es
I talk to myself and laugh
All is happ!ness that
Money cannot buy.

Then comes the storm and thunder
I got drums here and
It's a cage in return of l!ttle wage
Why so I always wonder.

My m!nd speaks, t!s not ma stage
For I know I belong to the
The table of poets, th!nkers and
ph!losophers, but for now
I'm stuck here
In the world of bloodsuckers.

Be!ng Real

I feel the whole un!verse ins!de my bra!n
Beyond T!me and Space bound
Ne!ther the fear to be lost
Nor the w!sh to be found.
I'm not a narciss!st
Ne!ther I pretend
To be a protagon!st
Walk!ng the down town
I see people sell!ng the!r soul
For paper notes.
Fake faces and sm!le
All over the places
No trouble, comm!t a cr!me
And blame the t!me
Being real is out of reel
It looks beaut!ful
Being real is out of trend
Though I tried harder to blend
But fa!led, feel!ng so low
My heart and mind explode
At the same t!me and
The ink bleeds w!th these
Executed rhymes.

Purpose of Poets

I'm in war w!th the words
Fight!ng battle of the vo!ce unheard
Each t!me I lost more than I won
And it goes on and on and on.
I seem l!ke th!ngs I didn't mean
People see me with eyes of laser rings
Try to spl!t my bra!n
Into two halves
But, my bra!n is already busted
In thousand p!eces
And a part of it is equivalent to
Hundreds of your dumb head.

A Typewr!ter

The typewr!ter type of wr!ter
A fcuk!ng error in L!terature and Grammar
A d!sorder in r!ght order
A metaphor, poet!c crim!nal
With marks on anonymous synonyms
An ace in the deck with clown head
Focused and stra!ght and when flow
You can't say no... no
Because a volcano with dynam!te
Black pen and paper wh!te
Brown sk!n, a s!n des!gned to win
Sharp collars touch and bleed
Pen and t!e are always my pr!de
The worst at its best
The f!nal Peaky Bl!nders
No classroom but... but
Librar!es and museum
Another br!ck in the wall
And to burn the un!verse
One matchst!ck is enough
And I've a full box.

The World of Humans

Black humans and wh!te humans
F!rst world humans and th!rd world humans
Super!or humans and infer!or humans
Religion humans and caste humans
R!ch humans and poor humans
L!sten all you demons in human form
If at once I slit your throats
There w!ll be flood.
A flood w!th one color blood
Red blood, red blood, red blood.

A Person

In everyday walks of l!fe there's th!s person
A person who took gunshot in the head just to educate young g!rls
A person who is an astronaut and lost l!fe in spaceshuttle d!saster
A person whose bones broken, face swollen still fight!ng in the r!ng just to br!ng a medal for the nat!on
A person who is sell!ng vegetables in the streets to feed the fatherless k!ds
A person who is bleed!ng on the deathbed to br!ng a new l!fe to the world
A person who is w!lling to go to school and learn but forced to stay at home
A person who has been abused and raped and dragged into world of prostitution
A person who is obl!ged to cover ha!r and wear long loose fitt!ng clothes to d!sguise f!gure
A person who is just 22 years old and d!ed in suspic!ous c!rcumstances allegedly due to p****e brutality
Fortunately I'm not that person
I'm a 21st century man who got the bra!n
From anc!ent and med!eval world trash can!

Poet's Shoes

Walk!ng the downtown
A clown w!th a crown
These spoonfed crowd
Heart cold and soul sold
Can't distingu!sh a d!amond among gold
W!th r!ches everyth!ng they've bought
St!ll orig!nality they can't afford
Don't have any clue
How it's l!ke in a poet's shoes
W!th !nk and paper his ent!re life glued
The top gett!ng h!gher and h!gher
The more that he cl!mbs
Bru!sed face hid!ng beh!nd the pa!nt
He's becom!ng fa!nt and fa!nt
Scream!ng on top of the lungs
Watch!ng h!s soul that burns
Tired of wa!ting for h!s turn
But the day that never comes
St!ll hold!ng on the courage
Pick!ng up the p!eces
Of h!s shattered dream
Blow!ng w!th the w!nd
Flow!ng w!th the stream...

Colorbl!nd

Stand out of the crowd
It is black or it is wh!te
I cannot rem!nd, but
Every time I look into the m!rror
I see I am colorbl!nd
I w!sh I could make it r!ght
And show everybody
Why is it to f!ght?
For we share the one world
And the same color blood
But, it doesn't work
Because ins!de each one of us
There's a demon
So, I dec!ded to p!ck up th!s pen
And ink an exorc!sm with alphabets
And end th!s rac!sm w!th
A death treat.

Fractions of Life

Fa!led in a Way

Fa!led in a way
A pol!shed man of words
These scrap papers and st!cky notes
Decent heartfelt thoughts
Words, letters and envelopes kept
Ins!de the box, some scattered in bra!n
Some are lost but w!th every page
Feels l!ke better than ever was

Fa!led in a way
A poet!c disc!ple
With B!ble and ink sn!per r!fle
Battle aga!nst t!me cycle
That cannot recycle
Truth may be inv!sible but unden!able
To one and to all
Death is the f!nal t!tle

Fa!led in a way
A fool, but not fake
Feel!ng, bel!eving and wr!ting…
The three m!stakes of the road that taken
A react!on equat!on of pen and passion
In black and wh!te fash!on
An imag!nation in creat!on
The definit!on of l!mited edit!on

L!bra

Pens and penc!ls and papers
Papers, penc!ls and pens
Like ink in the ve!ns
Graph!te in bones
And canvas is the soul
Thoughts ris!ng from deep down
Feelings fall!ng from h!gh above
Somet!mes gentle somet!mes bold
Like a l!terary rock and roll
The seventh of the twelve
And the only inan!mate object
That scale all other subjects
And reflects the beauty of
Love, peace and tranquil!ty
From the ar!se of the Ar!es
To the sea of P!sces
Str!ves to keep everyth!ng in balance
L!bra... not just a L!bra but
A l!brary of art, l!terature and poetry
Purely romant!c at heart
Mostly shy but never self!sh
Perfectly car!ng, lov!ng and forgiv!ng
But, even the!r pat!ence has a l!mit
And once the l!mit is crossed
They're a burn!ng volcano
Mak!ng others happy is the!r happ!ness
An epitome of loyalty and honestly
And a hater of injust!ce.

Feel

If you feel l!ke to feel l!ke a poet
If you th!nk l!ke to th!nk l!ke a poet
If you l!ke to walk l!ke a poet
Seize the moment and own it, be a poet
Fly away the world of doubts
Into world of thoughts
Wave away the world of troubles
Into a world of bubbles
Like lotus sprouts fall!ng from the clouds
The sound that is never loud
Like the pen roll!ng on paper
Metamorphos!s beg!ns from w!thin
Add color to your thoughts
Give w!ngs to your words
Qu!te like a poet... a qu!et poet
L!ke you, me, he, she and we
Anyone, anyone can be
Feel free to be free
Like b!rds, butterfl!es and bee
Make it happen and once it happens
It w!ll keep happen!ng...
Like the w!nd is blow!ng, ra!n is ra!ning
Sun is shin!ng, ra!nbow glow!ng
Birds sing!ng, leaves danc!ng
Everyth!ng surreal and enchant!ng
Like poetry in a pa!nting.

Pa!nting the Bubbles

A man and h!s w!fe
Stand aga!nst all odds
Work!ng harder and harder
T!ll sweat flows w!th blood
With the pr!ce of the!r strength
And age they made a boat
So the!r generation could l!ve in peace
But, in the sea of ev!l soc!ety
They are be!ng troubled a lot
The poor couple were sober
L!ke a sa!nt.
Now they're gett!ng older day by day
Everyth!ng is becom!ng fa!nt
Melting bones and muscles
And the!r generat!on
Pa!nting the world of bubbles.

Anonymous

Wear!ng a tie and pa!nted sm!le
Gett!ng h!red and be!ng f!red
L!fe is act!ng l!ke a wyle
Just a man differently w!red
T!red but self-insp!red
A sober who has colors and ink
Try to blend in among the crowd of bl!nd
But, fa!led and t!me sl!ps away
And after a year gone by
With canvas was uncovered
Found his dreams
Shattered on the floor
Like it was meant to be before
And deeply real!zed
For the whole t!me
People around h!m p!ctured h!m
Not more than a joker.

Ode to the Ra!n

The clouds set the stage
Thunder announces your glory
L!ghtning sparkles your way
A half str!ng of colors
Sets on the sky and touches the ground
The other half g!ves colors
To flowers, b!rds and butterfl!es
The wind took its chance
And makes every leaf dance
The b!rds open w!ngs so w!de
And s!ng the greatest melody
It is the!r h!ghest pr!de
I have heard pearls are in the deep ocean
But, I see them fall!ng from the sky.

If I Were an Alphabet

If I were an alphabet
I could be "P" from
Paper, Pen, and Peace
Or "O" from Ocean, Or!gin, Opera
Or maybe "E" from
Everything Evolves and Erased
Or possibly could be "T" from
Tie, Tea, and Tragedy
Or "R" from
Rainbow, Ra!n, and R!ver
Or can be "Y" from
Yellow, Youth, Years
Wh!ch on its own become
Phrases of Eternal Thoughts Rained on You.

Time Travel with Art

Art, L!terature, and Poetry
More l!ke a t!me travel
Etern!ty to infinty
It is not useless
It is just used less
For an art!st is blessed
Beaut!fool mess!

Not a Poet

Not much of a poet
No, not even qu!te a b!t these
Uncountable and unquenchable
Th!rsts keep com!ng
L!ke dust pa!nted with words
A Un!verse and
I'm not do!ng it, it's happen!ng

Scattered bra!n, thousands of st!cky notes
    ins!de the head mostly
D!sappeared, few f!nd a place
Black pen and paper wh!te
Yes black pen a paper wh!te
And I feel l!ke I'm infin!te
And I'm not doing it, it's happening

Every I found is noth!ng
And a new l!fe ins!de like
Deja vu, but m!rror and m!rage
Can never be fr!ends
And the tragedy rema!ned
Vis!on, creat!on, a miss!on
An art!st's terror!st
The offic!al m!sfit, and
I'm not do!ng it…
It's fcuk!ng happen!ng.

Apology to Beauty

A fool got involved
Revolv!ng the sun
T!me, pen and paper burn
A planet ins!de a planet
L!ke Romantic!sm sonnet
A mag!cian from Egypt!an and Ital!an
Cleopatra, Mona L!sa, Em!ly Dick!nson,
Lady D!ana, Mar!lyn Monroe
Amy Winehouse...
All the beauty been so low
All caught up in the web sp!nning them
I w!sh I could be Sp!derman
For Mary Jane I'm gonna save them
A l!ttle pure poet!c bra!n
Hold!ng honeybee, sugar and roses
His love, thoughts, words lotus pure
With s!ncerity wish peace and prosper!ty
A patent apology
To all lost beauty
For you all are a poetry
Liv!ng ins!de me.

Mag!c

With pen danc!ng on f!ngert!ps
Paper notepad on the lap
Gaz!ng towards the gl!ttering sky
A fool talk!ng to the moon
Thought to pa!nt it
W!th ra!nbow, you know
L!ke frozen snow.
The r!ver may stop but
Words and feel!ngs don't
A m!nd blown... vol - ka - no
Steal!ng my control from
Ins!de my soul
Because there's mag!c
In my sk!n and bones.

A Man's Fa!th

She asked "What's fa!th"
I repl!ed, com!ng back by walk!ng
Count!ng the star towards home
With a bag full of grocer!es
For dad, sister, and mom.
Fa!th is fool!sh
The w!ngs keep h!m rid!ng
With a sm!le on face
Every next day is less
Of the present day
A fool could be a poet
Or a poet could be a fool
Who knew... I do.
T!me and a!r we inhale
Is not for sale
Have to earn it bat by b!t
Pat!ently wa!ting no duplicat!ng
Always real in debat!ng
T!me has its own way
To present a present
Stay, pray and care
Until death
That's the man's fa!th.

Why So Ser!ous

Taktse beg!ns with 'T'
Ranjeet ends with 'T'
You see I'm that 'T' from poetry
T!me truth and Tragedy
For every fore f!nger on me
I've longest f!nger for them
The internat!onal symbol
An error in grammar and L!terature
Funny but so true
The Taktse of Tathangchen
A foolish JokeR who beats
Ace in the deck — checkmate
Slow l!ke a turtle race
Takes t!me to explode vol - ca - no
Against the guns and bombs
With paper and pen
I'm hand grenade
A paper plane w!th
Love and peace wr!tten on it
And I don't qu!t
T!ll the end.

Unseen V!sions

Every moment I speak to me
A v!sion comes, I can see
A new place and t!me awa!ts for me
What should I pretend to be
An employee in the c!ty crowd
A resource person for a better future
A s!mple man where the s!lence
Sounds so loud
But t!me and fate has its own way
And for now people around
I heard them say!ng
"A poet lost in the un!verse
Of words and thoughts".

The G!ft of Autumn

Sweet calm sunsh!ne
Light!ng the way to w!nter
The br!ghtest of the blue sky
And cotton candy l!ke clouds
Over my head, over my shoulder
And as far as I see
Into the colors of autumn
I see a bunch of cherry blossom
Pure, frag!le and whit!sh p!nk
Tiny petals l!ke dew drops
As soft as feathers of a b!rd
I feel the fragrance from m!les away
And when I come across I...
I... I just stand and stare in wonder
Why my words are not as beaut!ful as you?
Why I can't help but fall!ng in love?
Every season comes w!th a surpr!se
And for me the g!ft of autumn is
The cherry blossom
Like Keats my heart beats
And soul speaks
A th!ng of beauty is joy forever.

Ink Speaks to Me

It is not a truth
It is not a pretend
A gen!us in absurd
For he knows he belongs
To the table of poets, th!nkers and
    ph!losophers
But, for now he is struck
In the world of bloodsuckers
And when I asked — who is he?
The ink speaks: it was me.

Noth!ng 'More or Less'

Noth!ng is more prec!ous
than a feel!ng of be!ng cared for
And noth!ng is more worse
than a feeling of be!ng ignored
Noth!ng is more bl!ssful
than laughing together
And noth!ng is more m!serable
than weep!ng alone
Noth!ng is more joyful
than a feel!ng of be!ng treated as fam!ly
And noth!ng is more pa!nful
than a feel!ng of be!ng pushed away
Noth!ng is more lovely
than to be the one for someone
And noth!ng is more ugly
than becom!ng no one to someone
Noth!ng is more attract!ve than loyalty
And noth!ng is more horr!ble than betrayal
Noth!ng is more pr!celess
than creat!ng someth!ng out of noth!ng
And noth!ng is more useless
than destroy!ng someth!ng into noth!ng
Noth!ng is more extraordinary
than l!ving a l!fe of your dreams
And noth!ng is more ord!nary
than l!ving w!thout a dream.

Anonymous II

L!ke a smuggler of m!racles
Appeared out of the m!rror
A present to present, from
The future, heart shaped
Box of sm!les and laughter
Another joker in l!terature
Sincer!ty and integr!ty of poetry
Inbu!lt w!th a b!t of w!t
The ink of inst!nct
Flu!d in ve!ns and bra!n
Every molecule, every atom
Made of d!amond proton
Every thought is l!ke tick!ng t!me
    bomb explos!on on the
      canvas of l!fe
There's no second chance
Everyone l!ves only once
P!cture it, pa!nt it, dream it
Descr!be it, f!ght for it
Conquer the mystery,
Wr!te a h!story before touch!ng
    the deadl!ne of death
Do not just breath, l!ve.

Ode to October

Gentle warmness of the sun
And the br!ghtest of the blue sky
Is it a lump of snow or cloud?
I st!ll have a doubt
How well I remember
Like a dreamer sky surfer
Oh, dear October
You always make me bew!lder
The color of the autumn
Mar!gold, orch!ds and dais!es
Sunflower, daffodils and bell shaped lilies
Heart f!lled w!th
Sitt!ng bes!de the lake
Beneath a maple tree
A lost soul w!th w!ngs
Writ!ng a song for the halloween
The even!ng greets
w!th the feel!ng of w!nter
Gl!ttering sky and aurora and the moonl!ght
It's t!me for fam!ly and fr!ends
For a closer get together
With a perfect warm bonf!re n!ght
Oh, dear October
I adore you more and more each year
You've always been so wonderful
A del!ghtfool fool is very grateful.

www.ingramcontent.com/pod-product-compliance
Lightning Source LLC
Chambersburg PA
CBHW030232100526
44583CB00013BA/934